The Abolitionist Movement

CORNERSTONES OF FREEDOM

SECOND SERIES

Elaine Landau

Children's Press®
An Imprint of Scholastic Inc.
New York • Toronto • London • Auckland • Sydney
Mexico City • New Delhi • Hong Kong
Danbury, Connecticut

Photographs © 2004: Art Resource, NY/National Portrait
Gallery/Smithsonian Institution, Washington, DC: 22; Bridgeman Art
Library International Ltd., London/New York: 9, 38 (Library of Congress),
28 (New-York Historical Society, New York, USA); Corbis Images:
10 (Bettmann), 8, 11, 19, 25, 33 top; Getty Images/Kean Collection:
33 bottom; Hulton|Archive/Getty Images: cover bottom, 3, 6 bottom, 6 top,
14, 16, 24, 26, 34, 44 top left; Library of Congress: 31, 40, 45 right, 45
left (via SODA), 12, 17; North Wind Picture Archives: cover top, 13, 15,
21, 23, 29 left, 29 right, 41, 44 bottom; Sophia Smith Collection, Smith
College, Northampton, MA via SODA: 18; Stock Montage, Inc.: 20, 32,
35, 39, 44 top right; Superstock, Inc.: 5 (Christie's Images), 4, 30, 36,
45 center.

     Library of Congress Cataloging-in-Publication Data
Landau, Elaine.
  The abolitionist movement / Elaine Landau.
      p. cm. — (Cornerstones of freedom. Second series)
  Summary: Discusses the abolitionist movement in the United States,
from the time of the slave ships to the end of the Civil War.
  Includes bibliographical references and index.
    ISBN-13: 978-0-516-24202-6 (lib. bdg.)   978-0-531-20825-0 (pbk.)
    ISBN-10: 0-516-24202-4 (lib. bdg.)   0-531-20825-7 (pbk.)
    1. Antislavery movements—United States—History—19th century—
Juvenile literature. 2. Abolitionists—United States—History—
19th century—Juvenile literature. 3. Slaves—Emancipation—United
States—Juvenile literature. 4. African Americans—History—To 1863—
Juvenile literature. [1. Antislavery movements. 2. Slaves—Emancipation.
3. African Americans—History—To 1863.] I. Title. II. Series.
E449.L35 2003
326'.8'0973—dc22
                                          2003016937

I T WAS A WARM SUMMER DAY IN 1840 on a Virginia tobacco **plantation**. It seemed like every other day, but this one was different. The plantation owner had just sold a large number of slaves. That morning they were leaving the plantation for good. These slaves had been sold to a slave trader, who would ship them to southern Louisiana to be sold to sugarcane growers there. No one expected ever to see them again. Slaves on sugarcane plantations were often worked to death.

Mothers and children were separated, as were husbands and wives. Once the sold slaves were handcuffed and chained to one another, they stepped into wagons. It was not a moment anyone could easily forget. Children wailed as they were pulled from their parents. Wives cried out to God to protect their husbands. Some sang this hymn:

> *"When we all meet in heaven,*
> *There is no parting there;*
> *When we all meet in heaven,*
> *There is parting no more."*

This painting by Eyre Crow records his impressions of the slave market in Richmond, Virginia, where family members and friends were harshly separated.

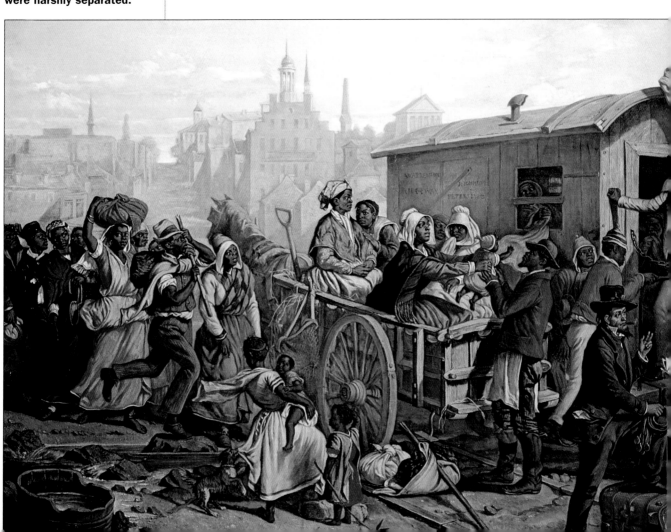

* * * *

Many slaves were needed to keep large southern plantations running smoothly. Without slaves, cotton plantations like this one would not have been successful.

OUT OF AFRICA

Before the Civil War slavery was legal in the United States. African slaves were brought here in massive numbers, as a source of free labor. The first Africans came to Virginia as early as 1619. Of the 6.5 million immigrants arriving in the New World between 1492 and 1776, only about one million were white. The other 5.5 million were Africans kidnapped from their continent and brought here against their will.

Slaves were viewed as property rather than as people. They were thought of in terms of their dollar value. White landowners knew that the abundant farmland in the South meant little if there were not enough laborers to work it. Slaves added value to a plantation. Slavery was an ugly, but very real, part of Southern life.

An abolitionist speaks to a crowd in Boston Common in 1835.

Slavery existed in both the North and South. This announcement was posted in Boston, Massachusetts, around 1700, advertising a recent shipment of 250 "fine healthy negroes."

TO BE SOLD, on board the Ship *Bance-Island*, on tuesday the 6th of *May* next, at *Ashley-Ferry*; a choice cargo of about 250 fine healthy

NEGROES,

just arrived from the Windward & Rice Coast. —The utmost care has already been taken, and shall be continued, to keep them free from the least danger of being infected with the SMALL-POX, no boat having been on board, and all other communication with people from *Charles-Town* prevented.

Austin, Laurens, & Appleby.

N. B. Full one Half of the above Negroes have had the SMALL-POX in their own Country.

Yet slavery didn't just exist in the South. Up until the American Revolution, when individual Northern states began to gradually abolish or outlaw slavery, slaves were used in the North as well. There they labored in various businesses.

However, the practice of buying and selling human beings was hardly accepted everywhere. Many Americans were against slavery and saw it as cruel and unfair. These sentiments can be traced back to colonial times, when people first began to speak out against slavery. Although these people were usually ignored, this began to change by the

1830s. Individuals with strong antislavery feelings insisted on being heard. They formed organized groups to advance their cause. Often their members published antislavery books and newspapers and held rallies protesting slavery.

By the early 1800s, every state north of Pennsylvania had passed **emancipation** laws to free the slaves. The institution of slavery was still strong in the South, however. Therefore, antislavery groups felt they had to do more. In some cases, the people involved even risked their lives to help slaves escape to freedom. These people had one common goal: to abolish slavery throughout the nation. Those who fought to put an end to slavery became known as abolitionists.

DAVID WALKER

Even though the organized abolitionist movement began in the 1830s, some believe it really started in 1829 with a man named David Walker. Walker was a free African American man whose father had been a slave. Walker wanted an immediate end to slavery. He wanted slaves to rebel if slave owners would not let them go. As an African American, Walker took tremendous risks in spreading his views. However, he never thought of himself as being as important as his message.

David Walker settled in Boston, Massachusetts, where he opened a successful used-clothing store. If he wasn't

ABSOLUTE POWER

Legally, a slave owner had nearly unlimited power over his or her slaves. This was supported by North Carolina chief justice Thomas Ruffin's decision in the case of *State v. Mann* (1829), in which a slave owner had shot and wounded his slave when she tried to escape. Ruffin determined that a slave owner could deal with a slave's misconduct in any way he saw fit. As the chief justice wrote, "The power of the master must be absolute, to render the submission of the slave perfect."

working at the store, he was usually out joining forces with other abolitionists. By the close of the 1820s, Walker was considered one of the leading antislavery spokespersons.

Unlike most white abolitionists at this time, Walker was anxious for change to happen quickly. In the 1830s many antislavery whites favored a gradual end to slavery. Their goal was to reason with slave owners, to change their minds and hearts. This strategy was known as **moral suasion**. If this didn't work, white abolitionists wanted legislation (laws) that would outlaw slavery.

There was much public support for abolitionists in Boston, where David Walker settled. Here, a large crowd of abolitionists gathered outside the Boston Court House in 1851 during a case involving a fugitive slave.

★ ★ ★ ★

Though African American abolitionists wanted to see slavery outlawed,
many wanted more for their people
than did their white counterparts. Most
African American abolitionists longed
to see their people take their rightful
place in society alongside whites. They
dreamed of a world in which blacks
and whites worked together as business equals, lived as neighbors, and
attended the same churches.

While white abolitionists wanted
to end slavery, some were not pre-
pared to fight for full equality for
African Americans. Not all were
ready to accept a totally integrated
nation, where blacks and whites traveled in the same
social and business circles and enjoyed the same rights
and privileges.

Even free blacks faced
discrimination. Here, an
African American is asked
to leave an all-white rail car.

Yet despite their differences, most abolitionists disagreed
with the views of the American Colonization Society. Organized in 1816, the society wanted to send all freed slaves
back to Africa, creating a new colony of sorts. Robert Finley, a Presbyterian minister, had come up with the idea.
Finley and his followers believed that African Americans
would never have a place in our nation's largely white society. He claimed that they would be much better off going
back to the "land of their fathers." After raising money to
purchase land, in 1821 the society bought the area now

Members of the American Colonization Society worked to remove large numbers of free blacks from the United States by sending them to Africa.

known as the Republic of Liberia, in western Africa. The group was only somewhat successful—just over fifteen thousand blacks were sent there before the Civil War.

Abolitionists felt that it was simply a plot to encourage slavery. They argued that colonization benefited slave owners. If slaves never saw a free African American, they would be less likely to rebel or run away.

David Walker frequently spoke out against any form of colonization. He noted that African American labor had helped to build this country and he urged freed slaves not to leave. Walker stressed that "America is more our country

* * * *

than it is the whites'—we have enriched it with our blood and tears . . . will they drive us from our property and homes, which we have earned with our blood?"

Yet David Walker is probably best known for a small booklet he wrote, entitled *Appeal: To the Coloured Citizens of the World*. The booklet, published in 1829, has been described as one of the most powerful African American antislavery documents ever written. The message was simple enough. Walker encouraged slaves to revolt against their masters. He wrote, "they [slave owners] want us for their slaves, and think nothing of murdering us . . . believe this,

★ ★ ★ ★

that it is no more harm for you to kill a man who is trying to kill you than it is for you to take a drink of water when you are thirsty."

Walker's stirring words gave slaves hope. His *Appeal* made them feel that they had a right to be both free and proud. Naturally, it was viewed less positively by slave owners. For them slave rebellions remained a terrifying possibility. They knew that they were outnumbered by their slaves. Even during small rebellions the slave owner and his family were rarely spared.

Abolitionist Henry Highland Garnet later republished Walker's *Appeal* along with a short biography of Walker's life. Garnet greatly admired Walker's work.

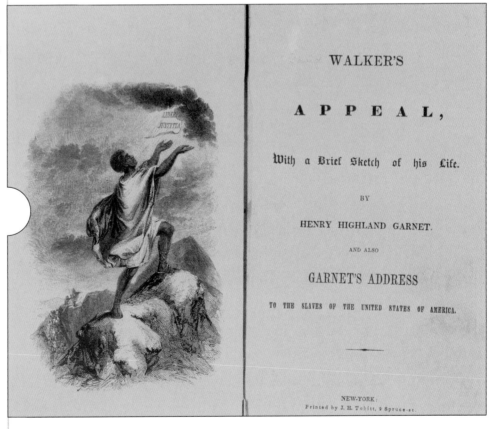

WALKER'S

A P P E A L,

With a Brief Sketch of his Life.

BY

HENRY HIGHLAND GARNET.

AND ALSO

GARNET'S ADDRESS

TO THE SLAVES OF THE UNITED STATES OF AMERICA.

NEW-YORK:
Printed by J. H. Tobitt, 9 Spruce-st.

David Walker managed to distribute his booklet throughout the South. His used-clothing business helped him do so. Walker sewed copies of the *Appeal* into the linings of the jackets he sold to free African American sailors. When their boats docked in the South, the booklets were secretly handed out.

Slave owners took David Walker's words seriously. They were determined to keep his *Appeal* from influencing their slaves. Louisiana, Georgia, and North Carolina passed laws to prevent slaves from learning to read and write. This stopped them from hearing the abolitionist viewpoint and helped to keep them in their place. It became a crime to teach even a free African American these skills. This trend spread, and before long, such laws became common throughout the South.

A price was placed on Walker's head: a three-thousand-dollar reward would be given to anyone who killed him. The amount would rise to ten thousand dollars if Walker were captured alive and brought to the South. David Walker was never captured or killed, though he died several months

Many slaves secretly learned and taught others how to read and write.

DAVID WALKER'S BRAVERY

Despite death threats and a price on his head, Walker refused to flee to safety in Canada. "Somebody must die in this cause," he said. "I may be doomed to the stake and the fire or to the scaffold tree, but it is not in me to falter if I can promote the work of emancipation [freeing the slaves]."

after his *Appeal* was widely distributed. At first, some said that he was poisoned, but it is now believed that he died of **tuberculosis**.

WILLIAM LLOYD GARRISON

White abolitionists did not always agree on the movement's goals and methods. Some wanted more for African Americans than did others. At times, the goals of these individuals were closer to those of the majority of African American abolitionists. One such man was William Lloyd Garrison. In 1831 Garrison began publishing *The Liberator*, his bold abolitionist weekly newspaper. He clearly stated his mission in the first issue. "I do not wish to think, or speak or write with moderation . . . AND I WILL BE HEARD."

Motivated by his strong religious beliefs, Garrison felt that no person had the right to enslave another. He also felt that African Americans should be granted citizenship and enjoy the same rights as whites. Garrison was one of only a few of the first white abolitionists to embrace David Walker's work.

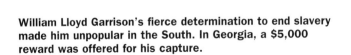

William Lloyd Garrison's fierce determination to end slavery made him unpopular in the South. In Georgia, a $5,000 reward was offered for his capture.

VOL. I.]   WILLIAM LLOYD GARRISON AND ISAAC KNAPP, PUBLISHERS.   [NO. 22

BOSTON, MASSACHUSETTS.]   OUR COUNTRY IS THE WORLD—OUR COUNTRYMEN ARE MANKIND.   [SATURDAY, MAY 28, 1831.

Garrison spread his ideas about abolishing slavery in his weekly newspaper, *The Liberator*.

He even published part of the *Appeal* in his newspaper. Garrison stressed that he was against using violence, however. As he noted in *The Liberator*: "a good end does not justify wicked means . . ."

Even though increasing numbers of local and national abolitionist organizations formed, slave owners remained determined to keep their slaves. They insisted that slavery was vital to the South's economy, claiming that without slaves the plantation system would break down. They also relied on **racism** to justify slavery, claiming that Africans were inferior and needed white masters.

ABOLITIONISTS AND RELIGION

The actions of many abolitionists were fueled by their religious beliefs. They saw slavery as a sin that had to be rooted out. Charles G. Finney, a Christian preacher well known for his fiery antislavery sermons, urged abolitionists on in their quest. He noted:

> "I had made up my mind on the question of slavery, and was exceedingly anxious to arouse public attention to the subject. In my prayers and preaching, I so often alluded to slavery, and denounced it, that a considerable excitement came to exist among the people."

15

Nat Turner went into hiding after the rebellion in Virginia, but he was eventually discovered and hanged.

NAT TURNER'S SLAVE REBELLION

Before long, slave owners began blaming the abolitionists for any problems that arose with their slaves. That included the rebellions slaves sometimes staged against their masters. One such rebellion, organized by a slave named Nat Turner, occurred in Virginia in 1831.

Turner, along with a small band of slaves, rode from farm to farm killing whites. More slaves joined them along the way, until their numbers swelled to about eighty. The state

militia had to be called in to put down the rebellion. By then, nearly sixty whites had been killed.

The state of Virginia and much of the rest of the South were shaken. Some wondered how much longer they could control their slaves. Virginia's state legislature even considered outlawing slavery, but most legislators voted against it.

Slave owners tried harder than ever to silence the abolitionists. They claimed that *The Liberator* had **incited** the Turner Rebellion. Slave owners hoped to stop Garrison's paper and all other abolitionist literature from entering the South. At one point, an angry group of slave owners even broke into the post office in Charleston, South Carolina, and destroyed bags filled with abolitionist **pamphlets**. In some cases, Southern postmasters began to cooperate with the plantation owners. They saw to it that abolitionist mail never reached its intended destination. Such pieces were repeatedly "lost."

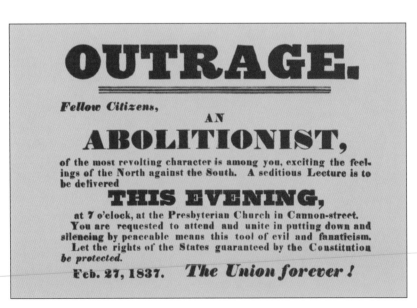

Signs like these urged slave owners to band together and put a stop to the work of local abolitionists.

★ ★ ★ ★

AMERICAN ANTI-SLAVERY SOCIETY

That did not discourage the abolitionists. In December 1833 the three most active antislavery organizations joined together with a group of free African Americans to establish the American Anti-Slavery Society. Garrison headed the group. At its first meeting, held in Philadelphia, Pennsylvania, the organization took the stand that slavery was illegal. Even if the Constitution permitted it, the abolitionists stressed that it was against the laws of God and nature. The American Anti-Slavery Society wanted all slaves freed immediately.

The Philadelphia chapter of the American Anti-Slavery Society was one of the largest and most effective groups of abolitionists. Its executive committee members are shown here in 1860.

Many white factory workers in the North feared that free blacks would take away their jobs.

As might be expected, the organization was extremely unpopular in the South. Nevertheless, membership in the American Anti-Slavery Society ballooned. Within two years of its start, 400 chapters, or groups, across the country had opened. By 1838 there were 1,350 chapters and more than a quarter of a million members.

Not all Northerners supported the society. This was partly due to racism. Though Northerners did not own slaves, they were hardly free of **prejudice**. Many believed the myths spread by Southern slaveholders and wrongly thought that a freed slave could never be their equal.

Another reason had to do with **economics**. White Northerners did not want large numbers of freed slaves to move to the North. They feared that these workers would flood the job market, and that might mean lower wages and fewer jobs for them.

★ ★ ★ ★

As publisher of the *Alton Observer*, Elijah Lovejoy printed news articles about both sides of the slavery issue. Pro-slavery mobs frequently tried to stop the paper's publication.

Therefore, when Garrison and other abolitionists scheduled speeches or rallies, there were often protesters in the crowd. Sometimes the abolitionists were hissed and booed. Eggs and rocks might be thrown at them as well. In some instances, mob violence erupted. Abolitionists such as Elijah Lovejoy were the targets of these battles.

Elijah Lovejoy was the editor of the Alton, Illinois, newspaper, the *Alton Observer*. In 1836 Lovejoy published an account of an African American who had been lynched and the subsequent **acquittal** of his white murderers. On three separate occasions after that, white mobs threw Lovejoy's printing presses into the Mississippi River.

Lovejoy's fourth press, a gift from the Ohio Anti-Slavery Society, arrived on November 7, 1837. The press was still in the warehouse when local slave owners learned about its arrival and demanded that Lovejoy turn it over to them. Lovejoy refused, and he and twenty of his abolitionist supporters remained at the warehouse to guard it. The mob smashed the warehouse windows, and shots were fired. Lovejoy was hit five times and died on the

Lovejoy died as a result of a mob attack on his warehouse. He was the first person in the United States to die in defense of freedom of the press.

scene. The mob tossed his press out the window and threw the broken pieces into the Mississippi River.

FREDERICK DOUGLASS

As the number of abolitionists grew, still more free African Americans became active in the movement. Among the best known and the most

THE DESTRUCTION OF PHILADELPHIA HALL

In 1838 an impressive building known as Philadelphia Hall opened in Philadelphia, Pennsylvania. The three-floor structure had been described as "one of the most . . . splendid buildings in the city." The hall was built as a place where abolitionists could hold meetings, lectures, and other events. Less than a week after its opening, an angry mob burned it to the ground.

Frederick Douglass devoted much of his life to ending slavery.

effective of these individuals was a former slave named Frederick Douglass. Douglass had escaped to the North and settled in New Bedford, Massachusetts, where he became interested in the abolitionist movement. Douglass was inspired by Garrison's newspaper, *The Liberator*, saying, "The paper became my meat and drink . . . My soul was set on fire."

Garrison was equally impressed with Douglass. In August 1841, when Douglass was just twenty-three years old, he gave a speech at the annual meeting of the Massachusetts branch of the American Anti-Slavery Society. Garrison immediately saw that Douglass was a brilliant speaker and hired him as a traveling **lecturer** for the society. Douglass became well known in the movement. His persuasive arguments and stirring speeches won over others to his cause.

Garrison and Douglass remained close for more than ten years but eventually went their separate ways. The men came to see things differently—Garrison's views were far more extreme than Douglass's. Garrison saw the Constitution as a proslavery document because it allowed slavery. Douglass felt that the Constitution was not necessarily proslavery. Believing that there was room for change, he

* * * *

thought that the Constitution might even "be wielded in behalf of emancipation." Douglass would later fight for the adoption of constitutional amendments to guarantee voting rights for African Americans, as well as other civil liberties.

Douglass was an inspiring speaker. A reporter from the Concord, Massachusetts, *Herald of Freedom* newspaper said of Douglass, "As a speaker, he has few equals."

INDEPENDENCE DAY

July 4 is Independence Day for white Americans, but African Americans were not free until slavery was abolished. In a speech entitled "The Meaning of July Fourth for the Negro," Frederick Douglass told a white audience that "this Fourth of July is yours, not mine. You may rejoice, I must mourn."

WOMEN ABOLITIONISTS

There were other unsettled issues among abolitionists as well. The role of females in the abolitionist cause was a hotly debated topic. Women were there when the American Anti-Slavery Society was formed in Philadelphia, but they were not asked to join.

Many women took an active role in antislavery organizations. In many cases, these campaigns often merged with women's rights causes.

* * * *

MEN AND WOMEN WORKING TOGETHER

At times, female abolitionists worked with their husbands or brothers to make a difference. Lucretia Mott, an outspoken leader of the antislavery movement, worked with her husband, James, to form the Free Produce Movement. This effort encouraged people to **boycott** products made with slave labor, such as tobacco and indigo for dye.

Lucretia Mott was a leader of women's rights and antislavery movements. She worked with Frederick Douglass and William Lloyd Garrison, among others.

At the time, society took a dim view of women involved in social causes. A woman was expected to remain in her role as homemaker. When a female abolitionist attempted to speak publicly on the horrors of slavery, she might be booed off the stage. Often people in the crowd would yell out, "Go home and spin!"

But female abolitionists were not about to do that. Both black and white women devoted years of their lives to ending slavery. At first, the women formed their own separate

This advertisement for the Free Soil Party supports Martin Van Buren for president and Charles Francis Adams for vice president in the 1848 presidential campaign. The party's slogan—Free Soil, Free Labor, Free Speech—is printed at the top of the ad. It reflects their opposition to the spread of slavery.

though related organizations. For the most part, these supported the activities of men's groups. The women raised money to keep male antislavery lecturers on the road and abolitionist printing presses running.

By the mid-1830s women demanded a more central role in the abolitionist movement. Females argued that while the fight to end slavery was important, women's rights mattered too.

The question came to a head at the 1839 national convention of the American Anti-Slavery Society. The majority of its members decided to permit the nomination of a woman to serve on the business committee. This caused a serious divide in the organization. Some felt that the group was going too far. These individuals left the convention and formed a new all-male group, called the American and Foreign Anti-Slavery Society.

Members of the American and Foreign Anti-Slavery Society further felt that the best way to end slavery was to elect antislavery candidates to government offices. To that end, in 1840 they formed a political party known as the Liberty Party. Later, in 1848 these individuals also joined with others to help start the Free Soil Party. This party's goal was to prevent slavery from spreading into the nation's new territories.

Meanwhile, women continued to become more active in the abolitionist movement. Like men, they made antislavery speeches and wrote abolitionist books, pamphlets, and flyers. Abolitionist writer Harriet Beecher Stowe published the novel *Uncle Tom's Cabin*, which clearly brought slavery's

Uncle Tom's Cabin reached a wider audience than other antislavery writings because it was published as a novel. The first 5,000 copies of the book were sold within two days.

135,000 SETS, 270,000 VOLUMES SOLD.

UNCLE TOM'S CABIN

FOR SALE HERE.

AN EDITION FOR THE MILLION, COMPLETE IN 1 Vol., PRICE 37 1-2 CENTS.
"   "   IN GERMAN, IN 1 Vol., PRICE 50 CENTS.
"   "   IN 2 Vols,. CLOTH, 6 PLATES, PRICE $1.50.
SUPERB ILLUSTRATED EDITION, IN 1 Vol., WITH 153 ENGRAVINGS,
PRICES FROM $2.50 TO $5.00.

The Greatest Book of the Age.

evils to light. The story follows the life of Uncle Tom, a faithful slave who is sold to several owners. Though his last owner beats him to death, Tom, while dying, prays that this cruel slaveholder will repent in the eyes of God and be saved. The book sold more than 300,000 copies in its first year and was translated into numerous languages.

Free African American women, as well as white women, worked hard to make a difference. Maria Miller Stewart was a free African American who gave abolitionist speeches throughout the Boston area. A similar effort was put forth by two white sisters, Angelina and Sarah Grimké. Although the sisters originally came from South Carolina, they spoke against slavery in a number of Northern cities. Sometimes they were jeered by the crowds. The Grimké sisters' actions were even publicly condemned by a group of New England pastors. Yet the women took the criticism in stride and continued their work.

Angelina (left) and Sarah Grimké (right) grew up on a South Carolina plantation. They often talked about their own experiences with slavery in their lectures.

THE UNDERGROUND RAILROAD

Other female abolitionists concentrated on bringing slaves to freedom. These women included some who worked on the Underground Railroad. The Underground Railroad, which was most active from 1830 to 1860, was not a real railroad, nor was it underground. It was a secret network of routes to freedom for fugitive, or runaway, slaves. During

Slaves secretly made their way from one safe house to another on the Underground Railroad.

their journey the runaways would rest in the homes and businesses of the railroad's "stationmasters," people who were willing to break the law to help slaves escape to freedom. There, they'd be given food as well as directions to their next stop on the railroad. The shelter and aid these slaves received helped ensure that they were not caught.

Underground Railroad "conductors" were individuals who went south to lead small groups of runaways to freedom. Some of these conductors were white, while others were African American. One of the best-known conductors was a black woman named Harriet Tubman. Tubman had escaped from slavery herself in 1849, but she made nineteen trips back into the South. Risking her life to do so, she guided more than three hundred slaves to freedom.

Many said that Tubman seemed fearless. She was known to carry a gun, which she sometimes used to threaten runaways who wanted to turn back. Tubman would point the pistol at them and say, "You'll be free or die."

QUAKERS—TRUE FRIENDS

Some of those who worked on the Underground Railroad were members of a religious group known as Quakers, or the Society of Friends. Quakers, who believe that all people are equal, were strong opponents of slavery. They hid many slaves traveling on the Underground Railroad despite the danger to themselves and their families.

Harriet Tubman proudly claimed that she had "never lost a single passenger" on the Underground Railroad.

TELLING THE TRUTH

Sojourner Truth, named Isabelle Baumfree at birth, was a former slave and an abolitionist speaker. She believed in equality for both African Americans and women. She once said,

"If the first woman [the biblical character Eve] God ever made was strong enough to turn the world upside down all alone, these women together ought to be able to turn it back and get it right-side up again. And now that they are asking to do it, the men better let them."

Sojourner Truth, born Isabelle Baumfree, changed her name to reflect her religious mission of spreading the truth about the sin of slavery.

It wasn't long before slave owners heard about Harriet Tubman. A forty-thousand-dollar reward was offered for her capture, but she evaded the slave catchers. Tubman continued to help black people any way she could.

* * * *

JOHN BROWN

Not every conductor on the Underground Railroad was female or even African American. White abolitionists were important to the system too. One white conductor, John Brown, was well known for his hatred of the slave system.

John Brown led a violent crusade against slavery.

Brown had been raised by a father who was fiercely against slavery. As an adult, Brown felt a special closeness to African Americans and often sought out their friendship. He longed to see real change in the lives of all African Americans.

Brown believed that violence was necessary to end slavery. He wanted large numbers of slaves to rise up against their masters in an armed rebellion. As a deeply religious man, Brown felt it was his calling to lead this fight for freedom.

He began by leading a few somewhat successful raids on plantations in Missouri. Yet that failed to bring about the broader success he'd dreamed of. So he set his sights on

This illustration shows John Brown leading an attack on the Doyle family, slaveowners in Pottawatomie Creek, Kansas, in May 1856.

Virginia and planned a larger attack. Brown started by putting together an "army" of twenty-one men. Sixteen of his soldiers were white, while the other five were African American.

On October 16, 1859, John Brown and his small army raided the government weapons arsenal at Harpers Ferry, which is now part of West Virginia. During the assault Brown and his men took ten hostages, one of whom was a nephew of George Washington. They kept these men barricaded with them in the engine house at the arsenal. Though Brown hoped this raid would be a major victory for his men, it wasn't. In the end, a group of U.S. Marines stormed the premises, overtaking the small antislavery army.

John Brown was wounded in the fight and taken prisoner. He was later brought to Charles Town, Virginia, where he stood trial and was found guilty of **treason**. Prior to being

★ ★ ★ ★

sentenced, John Brown was permitted to address the court. In this now-famous speech, he said:

"Now if it be deemed necessary that I should forfeit my life for the furtherance of the ends of justice, and mingle my blood further with . . . the blood of millions in this slave country whose rights are discarded by wicked, cruel, and unjust enactments, I submit; so let it be done."

John Brown was sentenced to death and hanged on December 2, 1859.

This illustration by Thomas Hovenden shows John Brown's last moments before his hanging. It was based on a fictional story that appeared in the *New York Tribune*, which described Brown stopping to kiss a black child in the arms of his mother.

Abraham Lincoln was
against the spread
of slavery.

Although John Brown was put to death, his trial helped rally public opinion in the North against slavery. Following his execution, he was hailed as a hero by abolitionists and others in the North while condemned by Southerners. Yet even after his death, John Brown's Harpers Ferry raid worried slave owners, who feared that others might follow his example.

DIFFERENCES DEEPEN

Before long, the tension between the North and the South on the slavery issue heightened. Slave owners were anxious to see slavery extend into the country's new territories as the nation expanded westward, while many Northerners were firmly opposed to this. In 1854 Congress passed the Kansas-Nebraska Act, establishing Kansas and Nebraska as two new U.S. territories. To the disappointment of many antislavery Northerners, the act did not outlaw slavery there. Instead it determined that the area's settlers would decide if slavery would be permitted. Southerners supported the act, while those opposed to slavery were furious.

To the dismay of slave owners, in 1860 President Abraham Lincoln was elected to office. The new president was against the further spread of slavery. In a speech Lincoln made on June 16, 1858, he had said, "A house divided against itself cannot stand. I believe this government cannot endure permanently half-slave and half-free." The fact that numerous abolitionist groups supported Lincoln worsened the slave owners' fears.

The election of Abraham Lincoln as president in 1860 sparked a desire for secession in the Southern states. Here, a crowd rallies in support of secession in Charleston, South Carolina.

Tensions mounted as the South increasingly felt that its economy and lifestyle were threatened. On December 20, 1860, South Carolina **seceded** from the Union. Within two months Mississippi, Florida, Alabama, Georgia, Louisiana, and Texas did the same. On February 9, 1861, these Southern states formed the Confederate States of America.

President Lincoln knew he would have to act to save the Union, but he hoped to avoid bloodshed. Then on April 12, 1861, the Confederates fired on Fort Sumter in Charleston, South Carolina, and took over the fort. At that point Lincoln no longer had a choice. The Civil War had begun.

Three days after Fort Sumter was taken, President Lincoln issued a

PRESIDENT LINCOLN'S VIEWS

Lincoln did not like slavery, but that did not mean he wanted full equality for African Americans. As Lincoln noted in a debate on September 18, 1858:

"I will say then that I am not, nor ever have been in favor of bringing about in any way the social and political equality of the white and black races—that I am not nor ever have been in favor of making voters or jurors of negroes, nor of qualifying them to hold office . . ."

The issue of slavery contributed to the onset of the Civil War.

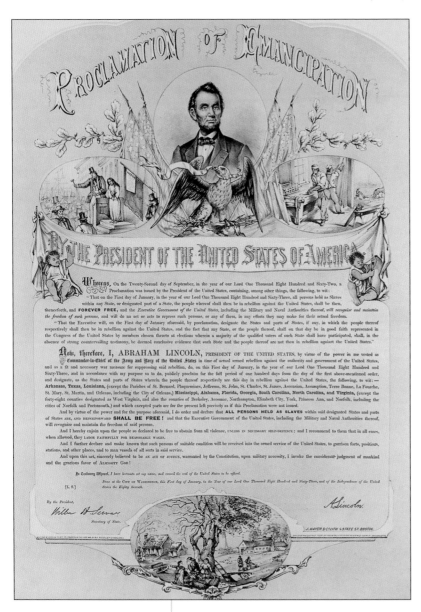

Lincoln's Emancipation Proclamation made it clear that one of the goals of the war was to end slavery.

proclamation calling for 75,000 militiamen. Soon afterward Virginia, Arkansas, Tennessee, and North Carolina also seceded and joined the Confederacy. A total of eleven states had left the Union.

The Civil War lasted for four years and marked the turning point in the fight against slavery. The battle to save the Union turned into a war for freedom. On January 1, 1863, Lincoln's Emancipation Proclamation freed the slaves in states rebelling against the Union. Later, in December 1865 the Thirteenth Amendment to the Constitution was **ratified**, outlawing slavery everywhere in the country.

A WORTHY STRUGGLE

Abolitionists had dreamed of an end to slavery for more than thirty years. They played an important role in making slavery a national issue, believing that it was a cause well worth fighting for. As Frederick Douglass put it: "Without a struggle, there can be no progress." The abolitionists' struggle helped to change the course of a nation.

AFRICAN AMERICANS IN THE CIVIL WAR

More than 188,000 African Americans fought bravely in the Union army, taking part in nearly five hundred battles. Twenty-three African Americans were awarded the Medal of Honor, the highest military honor given for bravery. Until 1864 African American soldiers were paid half of what white soldiers were; after that, Congress granted them equal pay.

NEGROES LEAVING THE PLOUGH.

Newly freed slaves celebrate the Emancipation Proclamation. It was the first sign of the end of a long struggle for freedom.

Glossary

acquittal—a judgement of not guilty

boycott—to refuse to purchase something, as a form
of protest

economics—having to do with money or wealth

emancipation—freeing someone from the control of
another person

incited—stirred up, moved to action

lecturer—someone who gives talks or speeches to groups
of people

militia—a group of citizens trained in military techniques
who serve in times of emergency

moral suasion—the belief that slave owners could
be persuaded that slavery was immoral and should
be stopped

pamphlets—small booklets

plantation—a farming estate where a large number of crops are grown for purposes of selling

prejudice—an opinion about a person or group (usually negative) that has no basis in fact

racism—the belief that a particular race is superior to another race

ratified—officially approved

seceded—withdrew or separated

treason—a crime against the government

tuberculosis—a serious disease affecting the lungs

Timeline: The Abolitionist

1619	1816	1829	1831	1833	1837	1840

| | | David Walker publishes his *Appeal: To the Coloured Citizens of the World.* | William Lloyd Garrison begins publishing his weekly abolitionist newspaper, *The Liberator.* Nat Turner's rebellion takes place in August. | The American Anti-Slavery Society is formed. |  | The Liberty Party is formed. |

| The first Africans are brought to Virginia. | The American Colonization Society is formed. | | | | Abolitionist editor Elijah Lovejoy is killed by a mob determined to destroy his printing press. | |

THE LIBERATOR.

VOL. I.]   WILLIAM LLOYD GARRISON AND ISAAC KNAPP, PUBLISHERS.   [NO. 22

BOSTON, MASSACHUSETTS.]   OUR COUNTRY IS THE WORLD—OUR COUNTRYMEN ARE MANKIND.   [SATURDAY, MAY 28, 1831.

Movement

1848 — The Free Soil Party is formed.

1849 — Harriet Tubman escapes from slavery and later becomes a conductor on the Underground Railroad.

1859 — John Brown's raid on Harpers Ferry takes place in October. Brown is hanged for treason in December.

1860 —

Abraham Lincoln is elected president.

1861 — The Confederate States of America is formed in February. The Civil War begins in April.

1863 — The Emancipation Proclamation frees slaves in states rebelling against the Union.

1865 — The Civil War ends in April. In December the Thirteenth Amendment to the Constitution is ratified, outlawing slavery throughout the U.S.

To Find Out More

BOOKS AND VIDEOS

Gelletly, Leeanne. *Harriet Beecher Stowe: Author of* Uncle Tom's Cabin. Broomall, PA: Chelsea House, 2001.

Landau, Elaine. *Slave Narratives: The Journey to Freedom.* Danbury, CT: Franklin Watts, 2001.

Lutz, Norma Jean. *Frederick Douglass: Abolitionist and Author.* Broomall, PA: Chelsea House, 2001.

Rockwell, Anne F. *Only Passing Through: The Story of Sojourner Truth.* New York: Knopf, 2000.

ONLINE SITES

National Underground Freedom Center
www.freedomcenter.org

Frederick Douglass National Historic Site
www.nps.gov./frdo/freddoug.html

Index

Bold numbers indicate illustrations.

About the Author

Award-winning children's book author **Elaine Landau** worked as a newspaper reporter, a children's book editor, and a youth services librarian before becoming a full-time writer. She has written more than two hundred nonfiction books for young readers. Ms. Landau has a bachelor's degree in English and journalism from New York University and a master's degree in library and information science from Pratt Institute. She lives in Miami, Florida, with her husband, Norman, and her son, Michael.